NATIONAL GEOGRAPHIC

Immigrants TODAY

Ann M. Rossi

PICTURE CREDITS
Cover (background) Chuck Savage/Corbis; cover (inset), 14, 16, 18, 24 (bottom), 30, 35, 36, 37 (bottom) PhotoEdit Inc.; pages 1, 22 (bottom) Corbis; pages 2–3, 11, 15, 37 (top), 38 (top and bottom) David R. Frazier; border (throughout) Corbis; pages 4, 4–5 Bettmann/Corbis; pages 6, 21 Catherine Karnow/Corbis; pages 8, 10, 33 (top and bottom), 34 (top) Getty Images; page 9 Robert Brenner/PhotoEdit Inc.; page 12 Owen Franken/Corbis; pages 12 (bottom), 13, 26 AP Wide World Photos; page 17 Nik Wheeler/Corbis; page 18 Eugene Schultz; page 19 Graeme Teague; page 20 Mexican American Fine Arts Museum; pages 22 (top), 23, 27 Lawrence Migdale; page 24 (top) Robert Holmes/Corbis; page 25 (right and left) Victoria and Albert Museum/Corbis; page 28 Rudi Von Briel/PhotoEdit Inc.; page 29, 34 (bottom) AFP/Corbis; page 31 Courtesy of the National Archives; page 32 Penny De Los Santos.

QUOTATIONS
page 7 *Coming to America: Voices of Teenage Immigrants,* by John DiConsiglio, pp. 44–45; page 9 *The Cuban American Family Album,* by Dorothy and Thomas Hoobler (New York: Oxford University Press, 1996), p. 37; page 15 "Lemongrass on the Prairie," *National Geographic* (March 2003); page 22 "Changing Face of Austin, Texas," National Public Radio *All Things Considered,* (February 29, 2000); page 26 "Literary Journal One of Few Outlets for Hmong Writers and Poets," *Saint Paul Pioneer Press* (November 20, 2000); page 32 "A Remarkable Trek to a High School Diploma for Sudan's 'Lost Boys'" by Chris Gray, *The Philadelphia Inquirer* (June 12, 2002); page 38 *The Uprooted,* by Oscar Handlin, (Boston: Little, Brown, 1973).

Produced through the worldwide resources of the National Geographic Society, John M. Fahey, Jr., President and Chief Executive Officer; Gilbert M. Grosvenor, Chairman of the Board; Nina D. Hoffman, Executive Vice President and President, Books and Education Publishing Group.

PREPARED BY NATIONAL GEOGRAPHIC SCHOOL PUBLISHING
Ericka Markman, Senior Vice President and President, Children's Books and Education Publishing Group; Steve Mico, Vice President, Editorial Director; Marianne Hiland, Executive Editor; Anita Schwartz, Project Editor, Jim Hiscott, Design Manager; Kristin Hanneman, Illustrations Manager, Diana Bourdrez, Picture Editor; Matt Wascavage, Manager of Publishing Services; Sean Philpotts, Production Manager.

MANUFACTURING AND QUALITY MANAGEMENT
Christopher A. Liedel, Chief Financial Officer; Phillip L. Schlosser, Director; Clifton M. Brown, Manager.

PROGRAM DEVELOPMENT
Gare Thompson Associates, Inc.

ART DIRECTOR
Dan Banks, Project Design Company

CONSULTANTS/REVIEWERS
Dr. Margit E. McGuire, School of Education, Seattle University, Seattle, Washington

BOOK DEVELOPMENT
Nieman Inc.

BOOK DESIGN
Three Communication Design, LLC

PHOTO RESEARCH
Paula McLeod, Worth a Thousand Words, Inc.

MAP DEVELOPMENT AND PRODUCTION
Bruce Burdick

Published by the National Geographic Society
1145 17th Street, N.W.
Washington, D.C. 20036-4688

ISBN: 0-7922-4560-1

Eighth Printing June, 2018
Printed in the United States of America.

Table of Contents

New citizens recite the Oath of Allegiance.

A family arrives in New York harbor in the early 1900s.

Introduction

The United States has always been a magnet for **immigrants**. They have come for religious freedom, for a chance to better their lives, and to escape from cruel governments.

Immigrants have come in three great waves. In the mid-1800s, millions of people arrived from northern and western Europe. Most came from Germany and Ireland.

The second wave of immigration was from the late 1800s to the 1920s. These immigrants came mainly from southern and eastern Europe. Most of them came from Italy.

Immigration slowed after World War I for two reasons. First, the United States government set limits, called **quotas**, on the number of immigrants who could enter the country. Second, an economic **depression** began in 1929. Jobs were hard to find.

After World War II ended in 1945, immigration began to grow again. Then in 1965, the government made it easier for people to come to the United States. By the 1970s, millions of people were coming. They all came hoping for a better life.

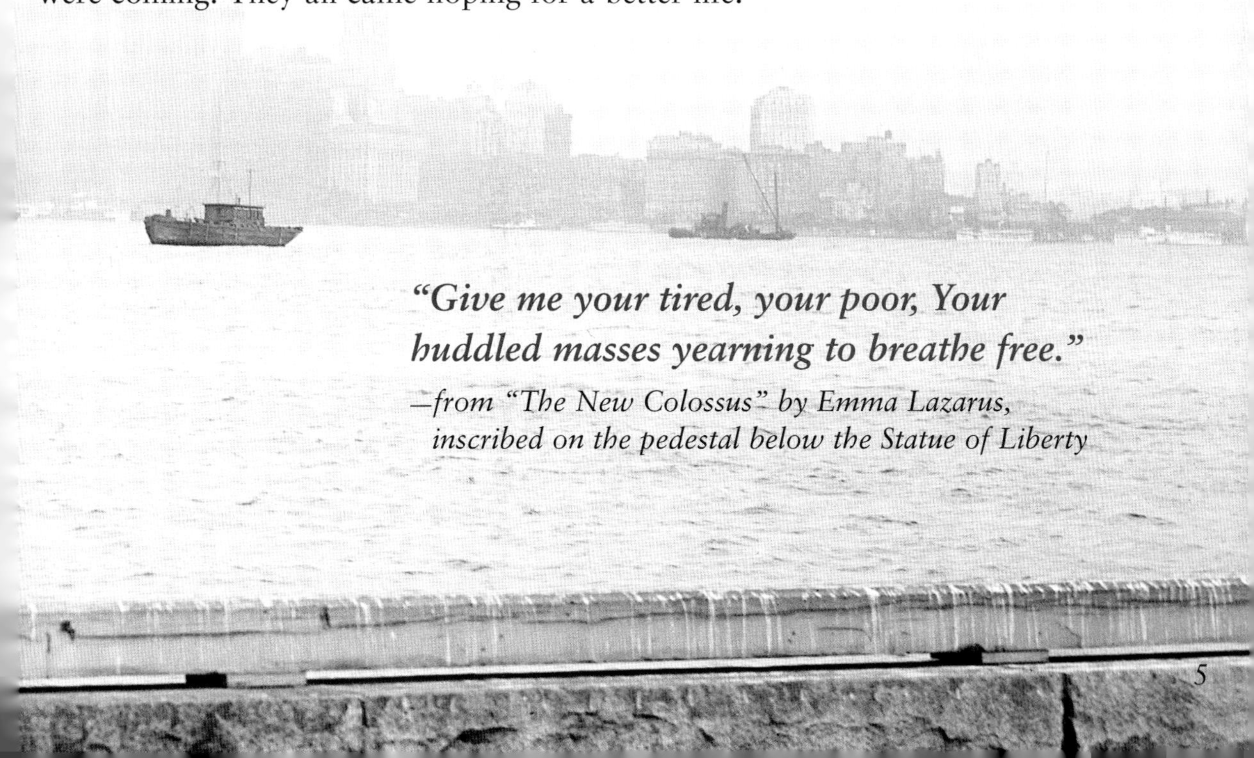

"Give me your tired, your poor, Your huddled masses yearning to breathe free."

—from "The New Colossus" by Emma Lazarus, inscribed on the pedestal below the Statue of Liberty

Chapter 1

Who Are the New Immigrants?

From the 1960s to the 1990s, most immigrants arrived from four areas of the world. These places are Asia, the region of Mexico and Central America, the islands of the Caribbean Sea, and Africa.

Why did they come? They came to get a good education or to get better jobs. They also came to escape war, starvation, torture, and death.

Vietnamese storefronts in California

Asian Immigrants

Millions of Asian immigrants came to the United States after 1965. Most of them were from China, India, Korea, and the Philippines. Most of them came to go to school or to get better jobs.

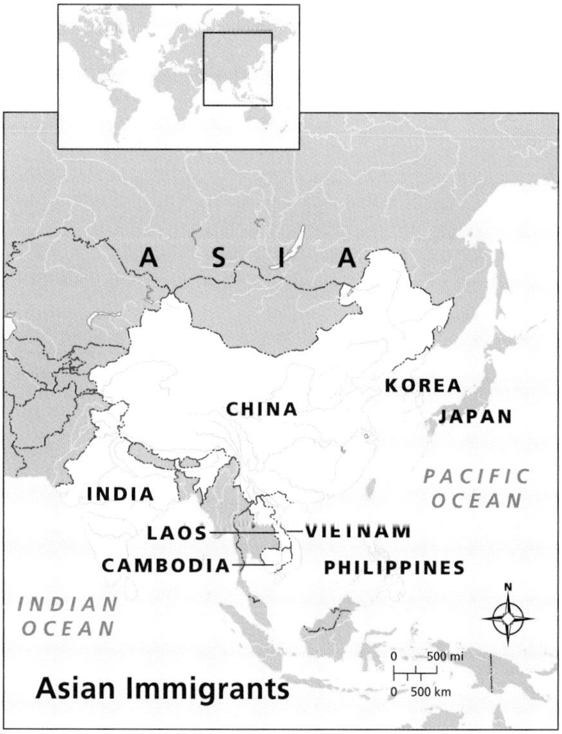

Other Asian immigrants came from Vietnam and Cambodia. These people were **refugees** (ref-yoo-JEEZ). They had to flee after Communists took over the governments of Vietnam and Cambodia in 1975. The new governments were brutal. People feared they would be put in prison or killed if they stayed. Special U.S. laws let many of these refugees come to the United States.

Before U.S. immigration laws were changed in 1965, few immigrants came from India. However, by the year 2000, there were over 1.5 million Asian Indians living in the United States. They had become the fastest-growing group of Asian immigrants. Many of them arrived on special **visas** (VEE-zuhs). These permits let skilled professionals work in the United States. Many Indians work in medical or high-tech fields.

Voices from America

"My parents tried to explain that under the Communist government my sister and I could never get an education. Most Chinese girls have less than an eighth-grade education. My parents wanted me to choose what I could do with my life."

—ELAINE ZHANG, Chinese immigrant

Mexican and Central American Immigrants

In the 1980s and 1990s, more immigrants came to the United States from Mexico than from any other country. One reason is that Mexico borders the United States. So, it is easy for people to get to the United States from Mexico.

Most Mexican immigrants came to the United States to work. Some came to the United States illegally. Today, they can become legal immigrants under a U.S. law that was passed in 1986.

Many immigrants came from Central American countries. Most of them came from El Salvador, Nicaragua, and Guatemala. Many of these people came to the United States to escape poverty. Others came because of brutal governments or wars in their countries.

Cuban immigrants

Caribbean Immigrants

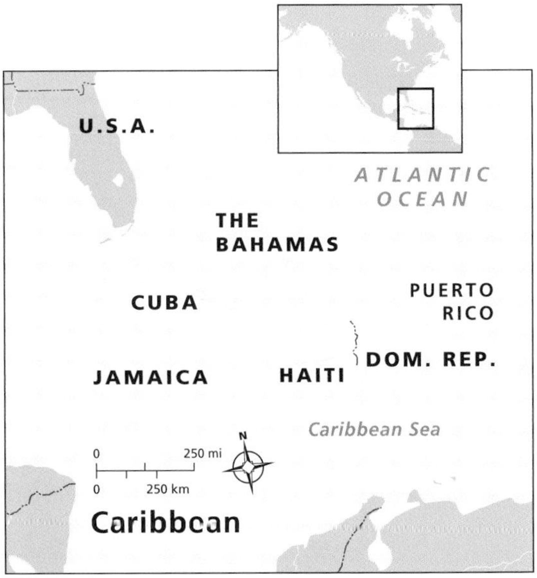

Millions of people came from the islands of the Caribbean Sea. Most of them came from Cuba, the Dominican Republic, Jamaica, and Haiti. They came to escape poverty and hunger. Many also came to escape being killed in their own countries.

Cuban immigrants began arriving after Fidel Castro became the dictator of Cuba in 1959. Castro set up a Communist government. He took businesses and property away from wealthy Cubans. So, many wealthy and well-educated Cubans fled their country.

Another group of Cuban immigrants began to arrive in 1980. That year, Castro opened the Cuban port of Mariel to anyone who wanted to leave Cuba. The people who left were generally poorer and less educated than the earlier Cuban refugees.

Some people from the Caribbean tried to reach the United States by boat or on rafts. Their long journeys were dangerous. They sailed through storms, hot sun, and sharks. Many had little food and water. Some people died trying to reach the United States.

Voices from America

"Finally, we've reached freedom."

—ROLANDO, Cuban immigrant, after escaping Cuba by climbing a fence to the American naval base at Guantanamo Bay in Cuba

A Jamaican woman

Children celebrate leaving a refugee camp in Africa

African Immigrants

Fewer immigrants came to the United States from Africa than from other places. About 500,000 African immigrants came to the United States in the 1980s and 1990s.

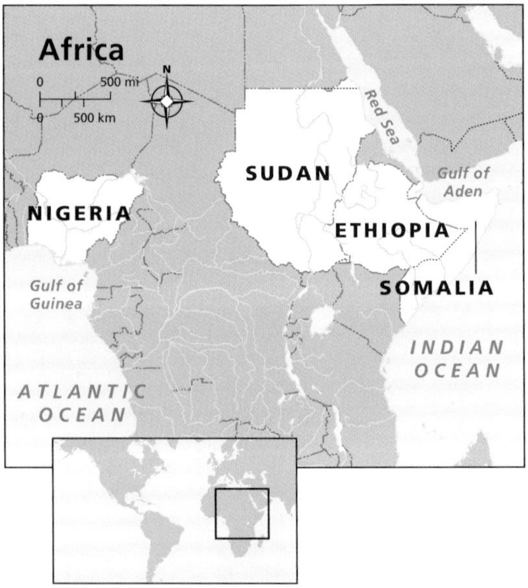

In recent years, crops in many parts of Africa failed because of **droughts**, long periods of little or no rain. Some people left their homes to escape hunger. Others left to escape war and bloodshed. Still others wanted to get a better education.

Most African immigrants came from the English-speaking countries in western Africa, such as Nigeria. many also came from Ethiopia, in eastern Africa. Ethiopia has had droughts and war. Other immigrants fled civil wars in Somalia and Sudan.

Becoming Americans

Chapter 2

Immigrants faced a number of challenges. At first, many knew little or no English. Even those people who were well educated were forced to work at jobs that did not pay well. They had to continue at these jobs until their English improved. Sometimes, people were as poor in their new country as in their previous one.

Some immigrants faced **prejudice** from people who did not want them in the United States. Other immigrants had religious customs that were different from the ones in their new communities. This caused problems if their new neighbors did not understand these customs. Some new arrivals once lived in rural areas. They had a hard time adjusting to city life in a new country.

Life in the United States was not always what newcomers expected. many succeeded in their new life right away. Some needed help.

Japanese and bangladeshi immigrants share their cultures in Boise, Idaho.

The Hmong of Southeast Asia

Many immigrants suffered greatly to reach the United States. The Hmong (hmawng) are among them. The Hmong people live mostly in the mountains of Laos in southeast Asia. When the Communists took over the governments of Vietnam and Laos, they began to kill their enemies. These enemies included the Hmong. Many Hmong fled their homes.

Most were settled in camps that **humanitarian groups** set up for refugees. Here the refugees were safe, but they couldn't go anywhere. Often, they were in these camps for a long time before they were able to leave. More than 150,000 eventually came to the United States.

A Hmong girl runs a vegetable stand.

Most Hmong settled in cities in Minnesota and Wisconsin. St. Paul, Minnesota, has the largest Hmong population in the United States. At first, the Hmong found living in the United States hard. Most were poor. They had little education and few job skills. The American way of life was very different from the life they had been used to. Soon, however, they became part of their communities. There are now hundreds of Hmong-owned businesses in the Minneapolis-St. Paul, Minnesota, area. In 2002, a Hmong, Mee Moua (MOO-uh), was elected to state government.

Meet | Mee Moua

Mee Moua fled Laos with her family when she was five years old. After many years in a refugee camp, the family came to the United States. She received degrees from universities in Rhode Island, Texas, and Minnesota. She became president of the Minnesota Hmong Chamber of Commerce. In 2002, she was elected to the Minnesota senate.

Many Somalis have found a welcoming home in Lewiston, Maine.

New African Americans: Somalis

Thousands of African immigrants came to the United States as refugees after fleeing their countries. Many were from Somalia. Most Somali refugees settled in large cities. Some of them found city life dangerous. They wanted to live in a safer place. They wanted better housing too.

Beginning in 2001, many Somalis moved to the small city of Lewiston, Maine. Lewiston quickly became known as a good place for Somalis to live and raise a family. The Somalis had a different language and religion from the people already living in Lewiston. At first, some citizens had problems adjusting to this large group of newcomers. However, the Somalis quickly put down roots. They learned about programs that helped them find housing, jobs, and medical care. Adults went to classes to learn English and to learn about American **culture**. Somalis also opened community centers and a **mosque**, a place of worship for Muslims.

Vietnamese Immigrants

The Vietnamese were one of the largest of the new immigrant groups. They began coming to the United States in 1975, at the end of the Vietnam War. At first, many American families and groups acted as **sponsors** for these refugees. As a result, Vietnamese immigrants were scattered all over the United States. Soon, though, they moved to places where there were already a lot of Vietnamese. Most ended up in California. Some went to large cities in other states.

Hundreds of thousands of Vietnamese settled in the Los Angeles, California, area. They opened businesses there. They also opened a Vietnamese chamber of commerce, an organization that helps businesses.

A Vietnamese doctor and his patient

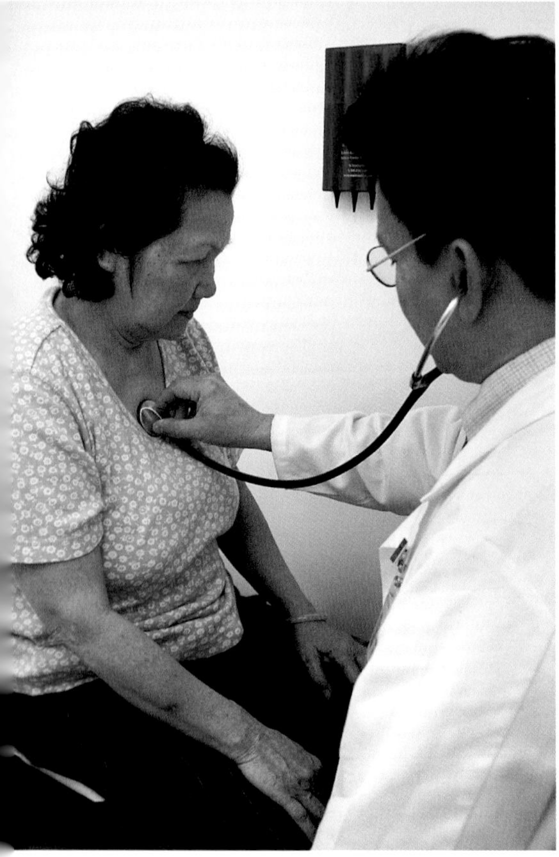

Many Vietnamese immigrants settled in Westminster in Orange County, California. Rents were low there. The immigrants moved to a part of the city that became known as Little Saigon (si-GON). It was named after Saigon, the capital of South Vietnam. Many Vietnamese opened shops and restaurants in Little Saigon. Today, the Little Saigon area has the biggest group of Vietnamese in the country.

At first, some of the people in Westminster asked the city to limit the number of immigrant businesses. However, the Vietnamese residents and business owners soon became an accepted part of the community. City officials named Little Saigon an official tourist attraction.

Oklahoma City, Oklahoma, has its own Little Saigon. About 10,000 Vietnamese immigrants live in Oklahoma City. They first arrived in the 1970s. A second wave came in the 1990s.

As new immigrants arrived, they opened Vietnamese restaurants, markets, and other shops in Oklahoma City. They also became doctors and police officers. Many immigrants continued to live in Little Saigon. Often their children moved to the suburbs after they grew up. They wanted a larger house, more open space, and a safer place to raise their own children. They had the same dream as other immigrants who came to America.

Voices from America

"I don't want to live in an old, small house. I'm living the American dream. We grew up poor. We want to move up in society."

—THUY, who immigrated with her parents to Oklahoma City from Vietnam and later moved to the suburbs after becoming a doctor

New Saigon Mall in Westminster, California

Cuban Refugees Settle in Florida

Most Cuban immigrants came to the United States as refugees after Fidel Castro became the leader of Cuba in 1959. Most of them settled in southern Florida. Florida is about 90 miles from Cuba and has a similar climate. Florida also had plenty of housing and jobs.

Little Havana, center of Cuban life in Miami

The first wave of Cuban immigrants had to leave most of their money and property in Cuba. Many spoke only Spanish. This made it hard for them to find the kinds of jobs that they had in Cuba. Many were professionals, such as doctors and lawyers. They had to go back to school and take tests before they could work at the same jobs in the United States.

Many Cuban immigrants took low-paying jobs. They worked hard and moved up to important positions. Others went back to school. Then, they got the same kinds of jobs they had had in Cuba. Still others started their own businesses.

Miami, Florida, has more Cuban Americans than any other city in the United States. Newspapers there are printed in Spanish. Television and radio stations broadcast programs in Spanish.

Many Cubans settled in a part of the city that became known as Little Havana. Some opened businesses. Others became bankers and executives in large companies. Few immigrant groups have become as important a part of their community as quickly as the Cubans in Miami did. Many Cubans have stayed in Miami, but others moved to the suburbs. Almost half the people in Dade County, Florida, are Cuban Americans.

A parade in Miami's Little Havana

New Multiethnic Communities

Clarkston, Georgia, is a **multiethnic** town, but it was not always that way. Not too long ago, almost all of the people who lived there were white or African American. Then, refugees began to move in. They came from Somalia, Sudan, Vietnam, Cambodia, Central America, and eastern Europe.

Buddhist temple in Milwaukee

These new residents changed the Clarkston community. They brought their languages, religions, and **traditions** with them. Students in the schools now come from dozens of countries. Many different languages are spoken. Some of the new people are Muslims, so they opened mosques. Some immigrants opened small **ethnic** shops to serve the needs of their community.

Towns in the Midwest have become multiethnic too. Until recently, there were few Latinos or Asians living in the Green Bay, Wisconsin, area. Then, Mexican and Asian immigrants began to arrive.

Many newcomers went to Green Bay to work in the meatpacking plants. Jobs were easy to find. Shops, churches, and community groups were set up to serve the needs of the immigrants. Stores sold ethnic products that had never been seen before in Green Bay. Green Bay became more **diverse** than ever before.

Wall painting in Miami's Little Havana shows Cuban immigrants.

Preserving History and Culture

Chapter 3

Most immigrants try to keep some of their cultural traditions. A community center can help them do this. A community center is a place for immigrants to get together. They can watch movies or listen to music from their homeland. They can share news about their homeland or celebrate ethnic holidays.

Many cities have ethnic museums or theaters. They give immigrant groups a way to preserve and celebrate their culture and history. They also give other members of the public a way to learn about another culture.

Some cities have tours that celebrate the **heritage** of immigrant groups. Miami has tours that help visitors learn about Cuban culture and history. The visitors see museums, art galleries, and monuments on Cuban Memorial Boulevard.

La Plaza de la Cubanidad in Miami is dedicated to people and places in the history of Cuba.

Bookstores also help immigrants stay connected to their homeland. A Hmong couple opened a bookstore in St. Paul, Minnesota. Their store sells books about the Hmong culture and history. It also sells Hmong crafts, such as special cloths, dolls, and clothing. The store helps Hmong immigrants to pass their traditions and history to their children.

Many immigrant groups have created websites on the Internet. Here, people can find information about cultural events and organizations. They can hear news about what is happening in the country they left. Young people can learn about the culture and traditions of their people.

The Mexican Fine Arts Center Museum of Chicago

The Mexican Fine Arts Center Museum is the largest Latino art museum in the United States. The museum shows prints and drawings by Mexican artists. There are photographs of important events in Mexican history. The museum also puts on concerts and plays by Mexican performers.

Family Traditions and Challenges

In many countries, grandparents, parents, and grown children with their families all live together. So, immigrants from these countries often tried to live this way too. However, laws in some cities limit the number of people who can live in one house or apartment.

Some immigrant groups have community structures that are larger than families. In Somalia, communities have elders. Elders are respected people. Other people in the community listen to them. Somali immigrants have kept this tradition. In places such as Lewiston, Maine, groups of elders often make decisions for the whole Somali community.

Many Muslim women wear a long robe called a chador.

Sometimes, family members come to the United States one at a time. To bring their whole family together again, many immigrants have to move from where they first settled to another part of the country.

Many immigrants come from cultures where children show great respect for their parents. Parents try to keep this family tradition in the United States. This can be difficult. School helps the children learn English and adjust to American ways. Often, children must show their parents how to do things. Family members struggle to find a way to balance traditional ways with new ones.

Many immigrants come from countries where most women do not work outside the home. In America, most families need two incomes to survive. So, the immigrant women learn English, go to school, and find jobs. Often, the families find this change hard to get used to.

Three generations of a Chinese-American family eat a traditional meal together.

Food

Most people want to eat the foods they are used to. However, immigrants cannot always find familiar foods. So, they soon open small ethnic grocery stores or restaurants. When enough immigrants from one country move into an area, large ethnic food shops open. These stores often attract customers from far away who buy foods they remember from their homeland.

Many immigrants avoid certain foods for religious reasons. Most Somalis are Muslims. They will eat only food that is considered *hallal*, an Arabic word meaning "permitted." Meat must be prepared a certain way to make it hallal. The first Somali immigrants could not find stores that sold hallal meat. So, they opened hallal markets in places where they settled.

Almost every immigrant community has its own restaurants. They serve familiar food. Other people enjoy eating there too. They like to share some of the tasty traditions of the immigrant group.

Voices from America

"One of the first questions that Indians ask when they move to a new place is where is the Indian grocery store and where are the Indian restaurants?"

—ANUPALM GOVIAL, an Indian-born businessman who moved to Austin, Texas

A Chinese New Year's parade

Festivals and Holidays

Festivals and holidays are important to most immigrants. They are a way for people to celebrate their cultural traditions. People eat traditional foods, hear familiar music, and display or buy handicrafts. Also, people from other cultures can come to enjoy new sights, sounds, and tastes.

Mexican Americans celebrate Cinco de Mayo (May 5). This holiday marks an important victory of the Mexican Army in 1862. Asian Americans celebrate the New Year with special food and fireworks.

Some festivals are small. A town might close off a block for a street festival. Sometimes, these small festivals grow. They become large and well known. Sometimes, people travel long distances to go to them. For example, Boston has a Caribbean festival. It has been held every year since 1973.

Celebrating Cinco de Mayo with music and dancing

Music and Movies

Music and movies are two ways for immigrants to share their culture among themselves and with others. Ethnic neighborhoods often have music stores. They sell music that is popular in immigrants' homelands. In cities, large music stores carry music from many different countries. Also, people can order tapes and CDs by mail.

Some large immigrant groups have radio stations that play music from their homeland. Radio stations in many states play Latino music. There is a Vietnamese radio station in California. Radio stations in New York and Chicago play music from different countries. Some radio stations also broadcast over the Internet. People can listen to the music of their homeland online. Immigrants also enjoy the music of their country by playing in or going to concerts.

In addition to radio, Spanish-speaking immigrants can watch many Spanish-language television programs. These include newscasts, game shows, soap operas, and other kinds of programs.

In some cities, it is possible for immigrants to see films made in their homelands. They can often rent these films. Or, they might see movies at film festivals that show Indian, African, Cuban, or Mexican films.

Movie posters from India

Latino newspapers on sale in Iowa

Newspapers and Magazines

Stores in ethnic communities often sell foreign newspapers or magazines. Immigrants like to keep in touch with what is happening in their former homeland. They can read about politics or sports teams. They can keep track of the latest music craze, or see what movies are popular.

Many ethnic groups have their own local newspapers. There are more than 100 Latino newspapers in the United States. Some cities have Chinese-language newspapers. These newspapers report about community matters and other important events. They also carry news from their home country.

Some magazines appeal to specific ethnic groups. For example, *Filipinas* is a monthly magazine for people from the Philippines. *Hispanic Magazine* carries features of interest to Latinos. Several popular magazines, such as *People,* are published in Spanish as well as in English.

One magazine directed to all immigrants is *Immigration Times*. It provides practical advice about living in the United States. It also contains articles about immigrant communities. Today, immigrants can find a wealth of information to help them learn about their new country.

Voices from America

"So many Hmong have no experience with life back in Laos. We need to document tradition and the change that's happening now, so we can understand the past and present, so we can better understand our future."

—KOU YANG, college professor and contributor to *Paj Ntoub Voice* magazine

Making a Difference

Chapter

4

Immigrants have always made big contributions to life in the United States. Recent immigrants are no different. They are in business and politics. They play professional sports. They are actors and entertainers, artists and writers. They go to school and work in factories. They drive taxis and work in restaurants. They pay taxes and serve in the armed forces. They are what people in any free country have a chance to be—good citizens.

Inspecting computer components at Texas Instruments

A hardware store in an immigrant neighborhood

Business

Certain types of businesses became popular with recent immigrant groups. Korean immigrants started hundreds of small fruit and vegetable stores in New York City and Los Angeles. In many cities, immigrants became taxi drivers. Then, they started their own cab companies. Farid Habibzai left Pakistan in 1990. He came to Portland, Maine. After working two jobs to save money, he started a taxi company.

Many Vietnamese immigrants have started successful nail salons. It is estimated that half the manicurists in this country are Vietnamese Americans. Kim and Thong Nguyen first settled in California. Then, they moved to South Carolina and worked as manicurists. Soon, they bought a nail salon. Then, they opened another one. Their businesses have many employees who are also Vietnamese immigrants.

Immigrant-owned businesses have brought new life to many American cities. Immigrants helped save the economy of Houston, Texas, in the 1980s. The immigrants stayed when other people left. They opened businesses. Don Wang, an Asian-born engineer, started a bank. His bank loaned money to Asian, Latin American, and African immigrants. Don Wang and his clients invested in property and bought homes.

Immigrants saved Toytown, an industrial area near downtown Los Angeles. This area was rundown when Charlie Woo bought a building there in 1979. Woo started a toy business. He bought toys made in Asia and sold them to stores all over the United States. The business did well. Charlie Woo and his family bought more buildings in Toytown. Other immigrants also started businesses there. Thousands of people now work in Toytown. Today, more than half the toys bought by U.S. stores come from Toytown.

Elaine L. Chao

Politics

Over time, many immigrants have won political office. It takes years for immigrants to become American citizens. These new citizens often do not register to vote right away. This can make it hard for candidates to get a lot of votes from their own ethnic community. For example, the Hmong started coming to the United States in the 1970s. However, a Hmong immigrant was not elected to state office until 2002.

Latinos have won city elections in many southwestern communities. Arturo Reyes was born in Tepetongo, Mexico. He became mayor of Lynwood, a city near Los Angeles, in 2001.

Elaine L. Chao became the first Asian-American woman to hold a cabinet post when she was appointed Secretary of Labor in 2001. She immigrated to the United States from Taiwan with her family when she was eight years old.

An Indian pharmacist measures medication.

Science and Medicine

Hundreds of thousands of recent immigrants work in the science and medical fields. Some came to the United States as children, went to college, and got advanced degrees. Others were already professionals in their country of birth. Many of them came to the United States under special programs for highly skilled workers. Some Indian immigrants came to work in the computer field.

Many Asian immigrants came to study science at American universities. Thousands of Asian Americans have gone to work as engineers in high-tech fields, especially in northern California.

Some refugees who come to the United States were doctors in their homeland. Thuong Nguyen was a surgeon in Vietnam when he came to the United States in 1980. Before he could practice medicine in the United States, he had to learn English. He taught himself. Then, he had to pass medical exams to become a family doctor. Finally, he opened his own practice in Oklahoma City. Many of his patients were Latinos who did not speak English. So, he learned Spanish. Four of his children also became doctors.

Education

Thousands of recent immigrants have become successful in the field of education. They are teachers, college professors, and school administrators. A large number of these educators came from Mexico, the Caribbean, and Central and South America.

Jaime Escalante became one of the most famous educators in the United States. A movie called *Stand and Deliver* was made about him. Escalante was born in the country of Bolivia, in South America. He taught physics and mathematics there before coming to the United States in 1964. When he settled in California, he could not speak English. He did not have a teaching degree. He learned English and got a degree in mathematics.

He started teaching at a high school in a poor area of Los Angeles. He helped his students do better in math than anyone thought possible. Soon, hundreds of students at the school were taking special advanced exams in math and other subjects every year. Jaime Escalante won several awards for his work.

In 1998, former President Ronald Reagan awarded Jaime Escalante (right) the Presidential Medal for Excellence.

Voices from America

"In America, our origins matter less than our destination, and that is what democracy is all about."

—RONALD REAGAN, August 17, 1992

A former Sudanese refugee in Michigan

Adults are not the only successful immigrants. Many young people have done great things. Some, such as John Manyok Tot, overcame hardships to graduate from high school. Civil war in Sudan, a country in northeast Africa, forced members of the Dinka tribe to leave their homeland. Tot left home when he was just five years old. He and thousands of children marched hundreds of miles to a refugee camp. Three years later, they marched to another one. Many children died.

Sponsors helped some children move to other countries. An American sponsored Tot and four relatives. Life in the United States was very different for these Sudanese. The teens had never seen a flush toilet or used a computer. Foods and customs seemed strange. In their culture, for example, it was rude to talk during meals.

Soon, Tot adjusted. He started high school in January 2001. He watched and learned. He graduated in June 2002. He and other children from Sudan have amazed people. They have done a lot in a short time. Many of them plan to go to college. Like Tot, they hope to help their people.

Voices from America

"A lot of people suffered. People suffered a lot of disease. We were walking using our bare feet. We didn't have shoes to wear."

—JOHN MANYOK TOT

Sports

Baseball is popular in Caribbean countries. Hundreds of immigrants from these countries play major league baseball in the United States. Pedro Martinez and Sammy Sosa from the Dominican Republic became two of the biggest stars in the major leagues in the 1990s.

Many immigrants played soccer before they came to the United States. Some were good enough to become professional soccer players when they arrived. Some used their soccer ability to become successful in other sports. José Cortez played soccer in El Salvador before he came here as a teenager. He became a kicker for American professional football teams.

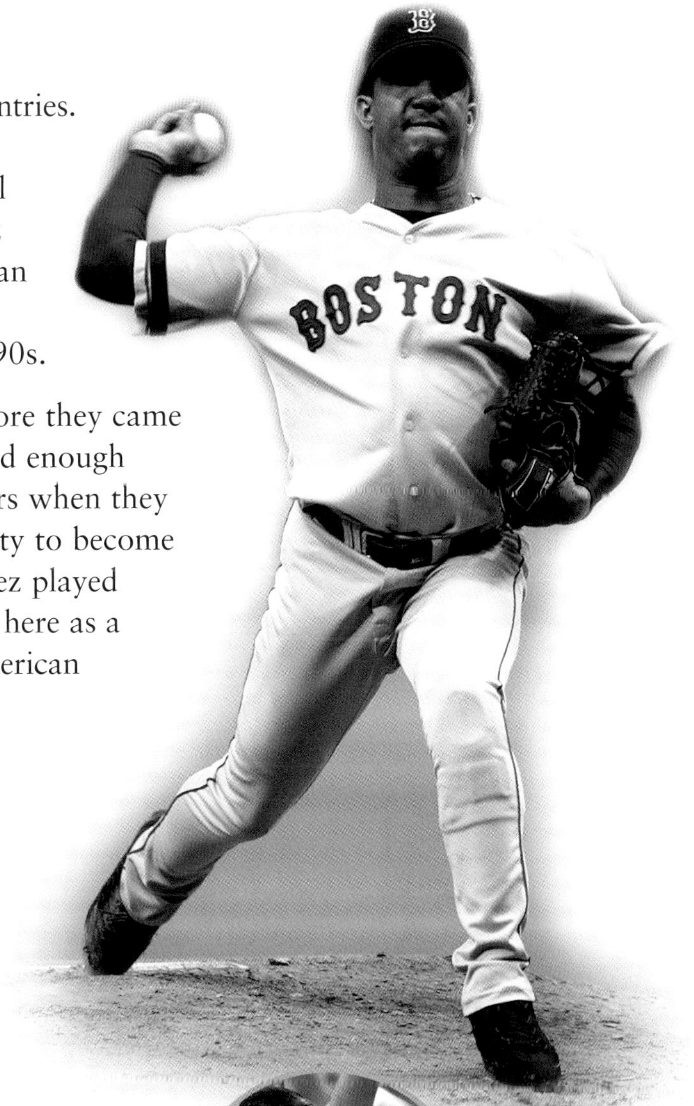

Pedro Martinez ▶

Meet | Hakeem Olajuwon

Hakeem Olajuwon played soccer as a child in Nigeria before he came to the United States. He settled in Houston, Texas, and became a college basketball star at the University of Houston. After college, he played professional basketball for the Houston Rockets for 17 years. He was known as "Hakeem the Dream." He became wealthy and bought a lot of property in Houston. He also started several mosques for Houston's Muslim community.

Cellist Yo-Yo Ma

Music and Entertainment

Entertainment has been the path to success for many immigrants. Some have become well-known television or movie stars. Many have succeeded in music.

Celia Cruz

Singer Celia Cruz was known as "the queen of salsa." Salsa is a kind of dance music from Latin America. Born in Cuba, Cruz left after Fidel Castro came to power. She settled in the United States. She recorded more than 70 albums.

Ruben Blades was born in Panama City. He studied law at the University of Panama. Then, he started playing with a band. Blades did not like the government in Panama. So, he left and came to New York City in 1974. Soon, Blades found a job in a band playing salsa music. Before long, he was recording salsa music too. In the mid-1980s, he moved to Los Angeles and became an actor.

Yo-Yo Ma was born in Paris to Chinese parents. He began to study the cello at the age of four. He came to America with his parents and studied music in New York City. Today, he is known all over the world.

The New Face of America

Chapter 5

Immigrants' lives have been changed by America. America has been changed too. These changes are reflected in schools, the workforce, language, and culture.

Schools

The latest wave of immigration changed American schools. Schools in large cities had always had students who came from different cultures and spoke languages other than English at home. This was not usually the case in small cities and towns. Then, immigrants moved to smaller communities. Schools there became diverse. Towns of just a few thousand people had schools with students from many different countries. In some classrooms, five or more languages were spoken.

Bilingual education laws have also changed many schools. These laws gave immigrant students the right to be taught important subjects in their first language. Many Latinos settled in the West and in New York City. These students could be taught in Spanish until they knew enough English to study and learn with other students.

A bilingual classroom

Latino skateboard shop owner

The Workforce

New immigrants work in all types of businesses. Many high-tech companies needed immigrants with special skills. Recent immigrants also work in agriculture, restaurants, hotels, and hospitals.

Some immigrants have taken low-paying and dangerous jobs that other people do not want. Mexican immigrants moved to the Midwest to work at dangerous jobs in meatpacking plants. For years, the New York clothing industry has depended on immigrant workers. Many immigrants work all night cleaning office buildings.

Immigrants have also helped bring new life to many cities. Some settled in rundown areas because housing was cheap. Then, they opened businesses and created jobs. Other immigrants stayed in cities when the economy was bad. They started businesses and helped cities get back on their feet.

Language and Popular Culture

In many places, you can hear and see the effect of recent immigrants on language. In cities, you hear many different languages. Signs on buses or in subways are often in more than one language. Notices in hospitals and public places are often in English and several other languages. Many government offices have translators. A town's Internet website may provide information for non-English speakers.

English Language Learners (ELL) courses for immigrants are taught in many places. Children may take such courses at school. Adult education programs often offer these courses. An ELL course may have students who speak many different languages all trying to learn English together.

Immigrants have also put their mark on popular culture. Supermarket shelves, restaurants, and bookstores all reflect the influence of immigration. Television and movies, art museums, and music all reveal that "American" popular culture has become a mixture of many different cultures.

Students learning English

Legacy

Every immigrant group has added something to American life. Each group has brought its culture and values to its new home and shared them with other Americans. These contributions have made American life richer.

Writers and artists have created works that reflect immigrant experiences. Sports figures, actors, and musicians have added their gifts to enrich American life. Ordinary people, who work hard every day, have helped to make their adopted country a better place for all of us.

Voices from America

"Once I thought to write a history of the immigrants in America. Then I discovered that the immigrants were American history."

—OSCAR HANDLIN, *The Uprooted*

This mural decorates a wall in a Vietnamese neighborhood in California.

Glossary

bilingual using two languages

culture the customs and arts of a nation or group of people

depression a severe decline of business activity resulting in high unemployment

diverse different, varied

drought a long period of little or no rainfall

elders older, important people in a community

ethnic of groups of people with a common racial, religious, national, or cultural heritage

heritage what is handed down from one generation to the next

humanitarian group an organization formed to help people in trouble or need

immigrant a person who leaves one country to live in another

mosque a Muslim place of worship

multiethnic relating to or including several ethnic groups

prejudice a suspicion or hatred of a particular group

quota a set number of people; immigration quotas set limits on the numbers of newcomers admitted from different parts of the world.

refugee a person who flees for safety to another country in times of war or disaster

sponsor a person or group that supports, or is responsible for, someone

tradition a custom or belief handed down from parents to children

visa an official permit allowing a person to come into a country

Index